Pebble®

Weather

Wind

by Helen Frost

Consulting Editor: Gail Saunders-Smith, Ph.D.
Consultant: Joseph M. Moran, Ph.D., Meteorologist
Associate Director, Education Program
American Meteorological Society
Washington, D.C.

Capstone
press

Mankato, Minnesota

Pebble Books are published by Capstone Press,
1710 Roe Crest Drive, North Mankato, Minnesota 56003.
www.capstonepub.com

 Books published by Capstone Press are manufactured with paper
containing at least 10 percent post-consumer waste.

Library of Congress Cataloging-in-Publication Data
Frost, Helen, 1949–
    Wind / by Helen Frost.
    p. cm.—(Weather)
    Summary: Simple text and photographs present wind, how it is formed,
and how it affects the Earth and people.
    Includes bibliographical references and index.
    ISBN-13: 978-0-7368-2096-7 (hardcover)
    ISBN-13: 978-0-7368-4919-7 (paperback)
    ISBN-10: 0-7368-2096-5 (hardcover)
    ISBN-10: 0-7368-4919-X (paperback)
    1. Winds—Juvenile literature. [1. Winds.] I. Title. II. Series: Weather
(Mankato, Minn.)
QC931.4.F76 2004
551.51'8—dc22   2003013407

Note to Parents and Teachers

The Weather series supports national science standards related to earth
science. This book describes and illustrates wind. The photographs support
early readers in understanding the text. The repetition of words and
phrases helps early readers learn new words. This book also introduces
early readers to subject-specific vocabulary words, which are defined in the
Glossary. Early readers may need assistance to read some words and to use
the Table of Contents, Glossary, Read More, Internet Sites, and
Index/Word List sections of the book.

Printed in the United States of America in Eau Claire, Wisconsin.
032013   007261

Table of Contents

What Is Wind?

Wind is moving air.
People cannot see the wind.
But they can see what the
wind does.

The sun warms the air. Cool air moves in and forces the warm air to rise. These air movements are wind.

Wind affects the weather.
It moves rain clouds.
Rain falls on the land
and water below.

Kinds of Wind

A light wind is called a breeze. A breeze moves leaves and grass. A strong wind is called a gale. A gale can bend trees and break branches.

A hurricane is a storm with very strong winds. Hurricanes start over the ocean and can move to land. They can blow down buildings.

14

A tornado is a storm with very strong spinning winds. Tornadoes can pick up animals and cars. They can pull trees from the ground.

How Wind Helps

Wind can help plants and animals. Wind carries seeds and pollen. Wind helps birds fly faster and farther.

Wind can help people. It lifts kites into the sky. Wind pushes people in sailboats.

People build windmills to catch wind. Wind turns the windmill. Some windmills make electricity. Windmills help people use the power of wind.

Glossary

breeze—a light, gentle wind

gale—a very strong wind

hurricane—a large storm with strong winds; hurricanes form over the ocean and can move toward land.

tornado—a violent, spinning column of air that looks like a funnel; tornadoes that touch land can destroy anything in their paths.

weather—the condition of the outdoors at a certain time and place; weather can be calm or windy; it can also be hot or cold, wet or dry, or clear or cloudy.

windmill—a machine operated by wind that grinds grain into food, pumps water, or makes electricity

Read More

Bundey, Nikki. *Wind and the Earth.* The Science of Weather. Minneapolis: Carolrhoda Books, 2001.

Eckart, Edana. *Watching the Wind.* Watching Nature. New York: Children's Press, 2004.

Schaefer, Lola M. *A Windy Day.* What Kind of Day Is It? Mankato, Minn.: Pebble Books, 2000.

Internet Sites

FactHound offers a safe, fun way to find Internet sites related to this book. All of the sites on FactHound have been researched by our staff.

Here's how:

1. Visit *www.facthound.com*

2. Type in this special code **0736820965** for age-appropriate sites. Or enter a search word related to this book for a more general search.

3. Click on the **Fetch It** button.

FactHound will fetch the best sites for you!

Index/Word List

air, 5, 7
animals,
   15, 17
birds, 17
blow, 13
breeze, 11
cars, 15
clouds, 9
cool, 7
electricity, 21

gale, 11
hurricane, 13
kites, 19
leaves, 11
movements, 7
people, 5,
   19, 21
plants, 17
power, 21
rain, 9

sailboats, 19
see, 5
seeds, 17
storm, 13, 15
sun, 7
tornado, 15
tree, 11, 15
warm, 7
weather, 9
windmill, 21

Word Count: 185
Early-Intervention Level: 18

Editorial Credits

Martha E. H. Rustad, editor; Timothy Halldin, series designer; Molly Nei, book
   designer; Deirdre Barton, photo researcher; Karen Risch, product planning editor

Photo Credits

Corbis, cover; Jim Zuckerman, 14; Richard Hamilton Smith, 10; Roy Morsch, 18
Digital Vision/Jim Reed, 12
Eyewire/PhotoDisc, 16
Index Stock Imagery/Henryk Kaiser, 1; Jan Halaska, 6
Unicorn Stock Photos/John A. Swearingen, 20; Tom McCarthy, 4; Travis Evans, 8

The author thanks the children's library staff at the Allen County Public Library in
Fort Wayne, Indiana, for research assistance.